fast fun & easy ®

CREATIVE FABRIC CLOCKS

6 Timely Techniques for Fabric & Paper

Lynn Koolish

C&T PUBLISHING

C&T Publishing

Text © 2007 Lynn Koolish

Artwork © 2007 C&T Publishing, Inc.

Publisher: Amy Marson

Editorial Director: Gailen Runge

Acquisitions Editor: Jan Grigsby

Editor: Deb Rowden

Technical Editor: Nanette S. Zeller and Gayl Gallagher

Copyeditor and Proofreader: Wordfirm, Inc.

Cover Designer: Kristy Zacharias

Design Director / Book Designer: Kristy Zacharias

Illustrator: Richard Sheppard

Production Coordinator: Tim Manibusan

Photography: Lucas Mulks unless otherwise noted

Published by C&T Publishing, Inc., P.O. Box 1456, Lafayette, CA 94549

Library of Congress Cataloging-in-Publication Data

Koolish, Lynn.

Fast, fun & easy® creative fabric clocks : 6 timely techniques for fabric & paper / Lynn Koolish.

p. cm.

ISBN-13: 978-1-57120-400-4 (paper trade : alk. paper)

ISBN-10: 1-57120-400-8 (paper trade : alk. paper)

1. Textile crafts. 2. Paper work. 3. Clocks and watches. I. Title.

TT699.K66 2006

745.593—dc22

2006025593

Printed in China

10 9 8 7 6 5 4 3 2 1

contents

dedication

To my mother, Ruth, for teaching me to sew when I was very young and for continuing to encourage me in whatever direction I choose to go.

To my husband, Glen, who is always here for me and is as obsessed with golf as I am with quilting—a perfect match.

acknowledgments

Thank you to:

Everyone at C&T for their ongoing support and enthusiasm

Linda Johansen for paving the way and teaching us all the wonderful fast2fuse techniques she uses for her fabric bowls, boxes, and vases,
and Laura Wasilowski for sharing all her fusing expertise

All the talented people who agreed to be a part of this book by contributing a clock: Patty Albin, Sue Astroth, Stacy Chamness, Becky Goldsmith, Wendy Hill, Franki Kohler, Kiera Lofgreen, Cyndy Rymer, Teresa Stroin, and Rose Wright

introduction

Even though I love the conveniences of the digital age, there is something classic about a clock with hands. I think that's why I started making clocks. And since I'm a quilter, fabric was the natural material of choice. With the introduction of fast2fuse, the clocks became even easier to make.

Once I started making clocks, I was (and still am) hooked. I can create any shape or size that I want. Clocks make perfect gifts because you can make something that suits anyone's personality or home (or both). It's so easy to make a special clock for someone.

When I first started making clocks, there were a lot of things I had to figure out: how to finish the edges, what to do if I didn't like the clock hands that were available, how to make sure the clock would hang properly, how to make dimensional clocks, and more. Now it's all here for you.

Tick tock.

Time's a wastin'.

Let's make clocks!

getting started

It really doesn't take much to make a fabric clock, and you probably already have many of the supplies and tools you need.

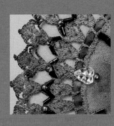

Supplies

clock movements

A quartz clock movement is made up of the battery-powered movement, a hanger, and the hands. The hands come in different styles, and you can choose to use a second hand or not. The stem of the movement comes in several thicknesses, from $\frac{1}{8}''$ to $\frac{3}{4}''$ or more. I generally use a $\frac{3}{8}''$ stem, except for clocks with lots of layers. You can also buy movements with a pendulum.

Clock movements are generally available in craft stores and woodworking stores (see Resources on page 48).

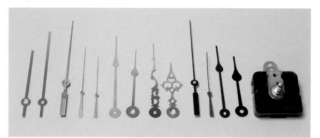

Clock movements come with different styles of hands.

Clock with pendulum

fast2fuse

The base material for most of the clocks in this book is heavyweight fast2fuse, a double-sided fusible stiff interfacing. It provides a stable foundation for a wide range of clock sizes and shapes and is easy to cut and shape. Fabric and paper are easily fused to the fast2fuse.

paper-backed fusible web

The easiest way to add fabric or paper to a clock is to use paper-backed fusible web (see page 12 for basic fusing techniques).

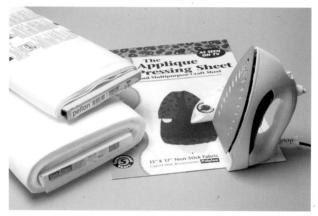

Fusing supplies

fabrics

The best fabric to use for these clocks is 100% cotton. It fuses well to fast2fuse and comes in an enormous range of colors and patterns.

easy!

Prewash your fabrics to ensure a good fuse. Unwashed fabrics sometimes have sizing or other finishes that prevent thorough fusing.

paper

Clocks are a great way to experiment with different materials such as paper. You can also combine paper and fabric—stitching, fusing, or gluing the combination as you would fabric. (see page 45).

Use fabric, paper, or a combination of the two.

glues

It's a good idea to have several types of glue on hand.

- ☐ Fabric, craft, or tacky glue works well for fabric and paper. When using the glue on a single layer of paper or fabric, apply it sparingly. When gluing layers of fast2fuse together, apply the glue liberally, but wipe away any excess that seeps out. It often helps to put some weight on glued pieces to hold them until the glue is set.

- ☐ Hot glue is great for applying trim and embellishments.

- ☐ Glue sticks work well when gluing paper to paper. You can also use this kind of glue to hold fabric in place until you stitch it down.

Keep a variety of glues on hand.

fast!

Hot glue dries quickly so it's perfect for hard-to-position trims and embellishments.

needles and thread

Many of the clocks in this book are quilted; quilting adds texture and helps hold fused pieces and layers together. The stitching is more decorative than functional, so you can use any type of thread you like: cotton, rayon, polyester, or metallic. Just be sure to match the needle to the thread type and size.

You can use all types of threads when making clocks.

paints

Use paints:

- ☐ On the edges of the clock pieces to cover the white edge of the fast2fuse

- ☐ On fabric or paper to tone down or alter the color or texture

- ☐ On the fast2fuse for an interesting texture

- ☐ On the clock hands (Clock hands generally are black or gold-colored. Paint the hands so they contrast with the clock or accentuate the color or design scheme that you're using.)

Use spray paint or any type of acrylic paint. If the acrylic paint won't stick to the clock hands, try using a base coat of spray paint.

Paints enhance your clocks in many ways.

easy!

To prevent clock hands from moving when you paint them, make a loop of masking or painter's tape. Place the tape loop on a piece of paper and place the clock hands on top of the tape.

Use tape to hold clock hands when painting.

embellishments

Embellishments add color, depth, and texture to your clock. Look for embellishments that are easily glued or stitched to fabric or paper and that don't stick up so high that they interfere with the movement of the hands. Anything that strikes your fancy or fits your theme is fair game. Find embellishments at quilt shops, scrapbook stores, hardware stores, flea markets, garage sales, toy stores, and all around the house.

Look for fun embellishments.

Tools

rotary cutter, ruler, and cutting mat

Use a rotary cutter, ruler, and cutting mat to cut fabric, paper, fast2fuse, and fusible web. Some people like to have a designated paper-cutting blade to use when cutting paper and paper-backed fusible web. Straight lines should definitely be cut with a rotary cutter (any size blade is fine). Many curves can also be cut with a rotary cutter, especially if you use the smaller 18mm or 28mm size.

Decorative cutting blades for rotary cutters are available in several different styles and are great for making decorative edges on fabric, paper, and fast2fuse.

fun!

Use a decorative rotary-cutter blade to make your own fusible bias to cover edges (see page 18) or to cut the finished edges on a clock (see page 31).

scissors

A good pair of small, sharp scissors with sharp tips is invaluable for cutting small pieces and sharply curved shapes.

craft knife

A craft knife, such as an X-ACTO knife with its small, sharp blade, is very helpful for cutting small intricate shapes, including numbers to mark the hours. Replace the blade as often as needed to be sure it is sharp.

circle cutter

A circle cutter is handy for cutting perfect circles from 1″ to about 8″. When you use one, be sure the blade is sharp. There are many varieties available; check quilt shops, scrapbook stores, and art supply stores for options.

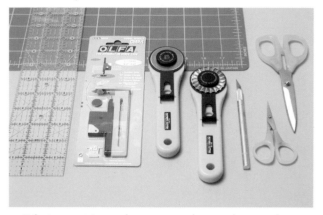

Whatever cutting tools you use, make sure they are sharp.

compass

Compasses are tools for drawing perfect circles. A regular drawing compass is fine for small circles (generally up to about 10″). For bigger circles, buy compass points that attach to a ruler or yardstick—these are sometimes called trammel points or yardstick compasses; find them at art supply stores, woodworking stores, and sometimes quilt stores.

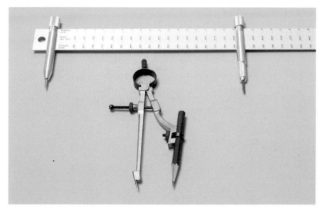

Use a compass to make perfect circles.

basics

A few basic techniques are used for all the projects in this book. Review them now, then refer back to them as needed while you are making your clock.

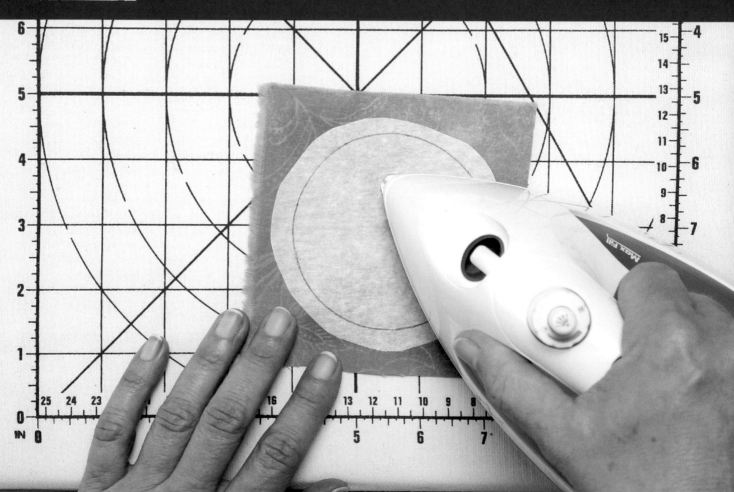

Fusing and Gluing

Because your clock won't be handled much and certainly won't have to go through the wash, fusing and gluing are quick and easy ways to put a clock together.

using fast2fuse with fabric or paper

Fusing fabric or paper to fast2fuse is a snap. Simply place the fabric or paper on the fast2fuse and press with a hot iron until the fabric or paper is thoroughly fused. This usually takes about ten seconds of firm iron pressure. I use steam when I am working with fabric, and no steam when I'm working with paper. If you want to make sure the fabric is placed correctly and doesn't slip, tack it in place first by lightly ironing the fabric or paper to the fast2fuse for about two seconds.

1. Draw or trace the shapes onto fast2fuse and cut out the shape on the drawn line.

easy!

Tape patterns on a light box or bright window and place the fast2fuse on top to trace.

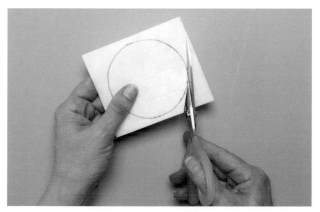

Cut out the fast2fuse on the drawn line.

2. Cut the backing and front fabrics or paper slightly larger than the fast2fuse shape.

3. Fuse the backing fabric or paper to one side of the fast2fuse. I suggest protecting your ironing board with a nonstick appliqué sheet when fusing.

4. Trim the backing to size using the fast2fuse as a guide.

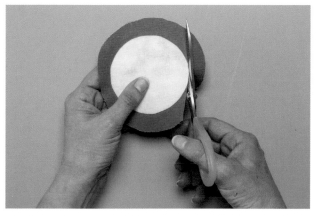

Cut out the shape using the fast2fuse as a guide.

5. Fuse the front fabric or paper to the front side of the fast2fuse.

6. Use the fast2fuse as a guide to trim the fabric or paper to size.

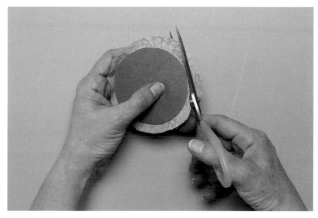

Cut out the shape.

easy!

Always iron the backing fabric or paper to the fast2fuse first. Then iron the fabric or paper to the front without any worries.

using layers of fast2fuse

Some of the clocks are made with multiple layers of fast2fuse. Use glue (see Glues, page 7) to make sure the layers of fast2fuse stick together. Fuse your selected fabric or paper to one side of each layer of the fast2fuse, then use a tacky glue to glue the layers together. Even if you are stitching layers together, gluing them first will hold them in place and add stability to your clock.

using fusible web with fabric or paper

Using paper-backed fusible web is a quick and easy way to adhere fabric or paper. It also prevents raw edges of fabric from fraying, so it's not necessary to finish the edges if you don't want to. I prefer Wonder Under by Pellon. It adheres well and doesn't gum up the needle if you sew through it.

Here's the basic technique for using fusible web on either fabric or paper.

1. Draw or trace the shape onto the paper side of paper-backed fusible web and cut out the shape about ¼˝ outside the drawn line.

Note: For asymmetrical shapes, trace the shape in reverse on the fusible's paper-backing.

2. Iron the fusible web to the back side of the fabric or paper. I suggest protecting your ironing board with a nonstick appliqué sheet when fusing.

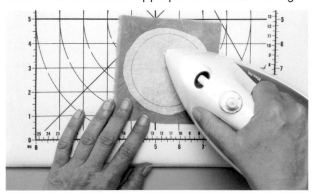

Cut out the fusible web ¼˝ outside the drawn line and iron on the back of the fabric.

3. Cut out the fused shape on the drawn line. Peel off the paper backing and the shape is ready to use.

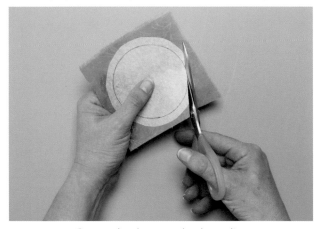

Cut out the shape on the drawn line.

easy!

When using fusible web, save the paper backing—also called release paper. Fusible web won't stick to it, so you can use it as a pressing sheet or to protect your ironing board.

using glue

A wide range of glues are available. Check your craft or fabric store, and be sure to read the label of the glue to make sure it is appropriate for what you are gluing. For fabric, paper, and fast2fuse, select a tacky glue or glue designed for fabric and paper. For metal or plastic embellishments, find a glue that works on those surfaces.

Marking the Hours

It's not necessary to mark the hours on a clock—it's still easy to tell the time without them. But marking the hours, whether you use numbers or shapes, can add personality to your clock. If the hour markings distract from the overall design, then don't use them. If, however, they are a key element of the design, then by all means play them up.

The hours are placed at 30° increments around a 360° circle. The easiest way to get correct placement is to use the Hours Placement Guide on pullout 1 at the back of the book. Make a copy of the Guide and use it for accurate hour placement. Cut your copy of the Guide to the size you need.

1. Line up the center of the Hours Placement Guide with the center of your clock.

easy!

If you forget to mark the center of a circle when you draw it, the quickest way to find it again is to trace around the circle onto a piece of paper, then cut it out and fold it in quarters. Place the folded paper on your circle and mark the center.

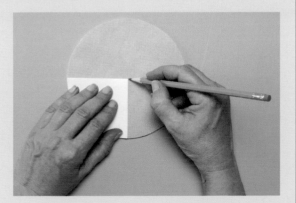

Use a folded circle to find the center.

2. Indicate the hour placement by making a light mark at the outer edge of the Guide at each spoke.

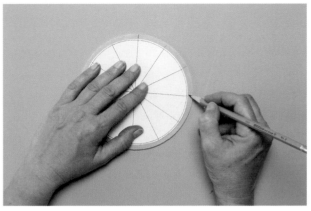

Center the Hours Placement Guide and lightly mark the hours.

You don't have to mark all the hours—you can mark just 3, 6, 9, and 12 o'clock. You can also do something a little different for those hours if you choose to mark all the hours.

fast!

Use a straight pin to hold the Hours Placement Guide in place when marking the hours.

Embellishing

Part of the fun of making your own clock is embellishing it. You can use anything you can attach to the clock that doesn't interfere with the movement of the hands.

Clock hands are available in a fairly limited range of colors and styles. It's difficult to make your own from scratch because they need to fit onto the stem of the clock movement in a very specific way. But that doesn't mean you can't embellish them. Embellishment can include painting the hands; gluing paper, foam, or metal shapes to them; bending them; and, well, you get the picture.

Embellish your clock hands to fit the style of your clock.

Quilting

Fabric clocks don't need to be quilted, but quilting is a fun way to add color and texture to enhance your design. Quilting holds pieces of your clock together and can be used to mark the hours.

Use quilting to enhance your clock design.

Printing on Fabric

Use your inkjet printer to print directly onto pretreated fabric sheets for a fast and easy way to create clock faces, backgrounds, and other elements for your clocks. You can even make the entire clock by printing on fabric (see page 44). Buy the pretreated sheets at a fabric or quilt shop or buy them online (see Resources on page 48).

Finishing the Edges

The edges of a clock can be finished at various stages of clock-making. In some cases it doesn't matter when you apply the edge finish; in other cases, it does matter. If the clock has hour markings or embellishments that stick up and would get in the way of a sewing machine or iron, finish the edges before you apply anything that would get in the way. However, if you plan to glue an edge finish such as cording to your clock, it's often best to leave that for last.

There are many ways to finish the edges of a fabric or paper clock. Pick one that fits the style of clock you are making, or make up your own edge finish.

easy!

The easiest edge finish is none at all. If the white edges of the fast2fuse work with your clock, you can leave them alone.

satin stitching

Satin stitching is simply a tight zigzag machine stitch. To get a clean, smooth edge, plan on making several passes to build up the layers of thread. Start with a narrow stitch that is not too tight—try a length of 1.0 and a width of 2.0. Make a second pass with the length at .8 and the width at 2.5. If you want denser coverage, do a final pass with the length at .6 and the width at 3.0.

fun!

Use a variegated thread when satin stitching for a varied look.

Satin stitching covers the raw edges.

painting

Use fabric or acrylic paints to cover the white edges of the fast2fuse. Use a color that blends well with the fabric or paper of the clock, or pick something that stands out and highlights the edges.

I've found it easiest to paint the fast2fuse after I've cut out the shape but **before** I fuse the fabric to it. Be sure to keep the paint on the edge—paint that goes past the edge may show through if the paint is dark and the fabric is light.

Paint the edges for a clean look.

cording or rickrack

Stitch or glue cording or decorative yarn to the edges of the fast2fuse for an added dimension. Use any type of cording, yarn, rickrack, or string that fits the style or theme of your clock.

fun!

Try twisting two or three lengths of cording for a dimensional look.

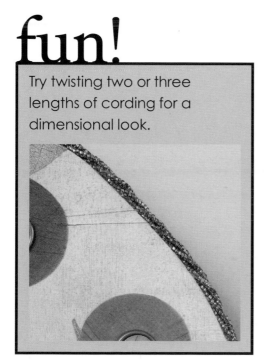

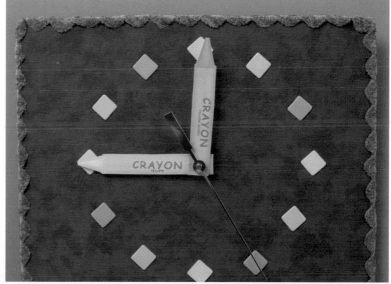

Cording, yarn, or rickrack adds dimension to the edges of your clock.

binding
Traditional Quilt Binding

Traditional quilt bindings work well for some types of clocks. Add flat or corded piping for another touch of color. (See page 46 for instructions on traditional quilt bindings.)

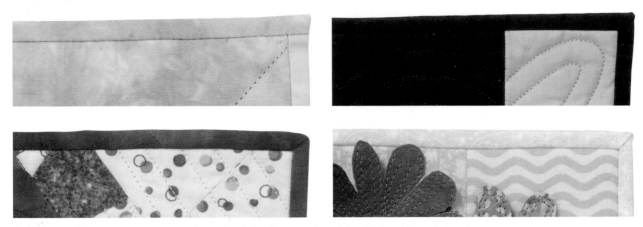

Traditional quilt bindings work well for clocks with straight edges.

Fused Binding

I first learned about fused bindings from Laura Wasilowski, who uses them to bind her fused quilts. They are a quick and easy way to finish the edges of a clock. Cut them with a regular rotary cutter or one with a decorative blade. (See page 46 for instructions on fused bindings.)

Fused bindings are quick and easy.

folded-over edge

Cutting the front fabric larger than the fast2fuse and folding it to the back gives a clean, smooth edge. This technique works on straight or gently curved edges. (See page 47 for instructions on making a folded-over edge.)

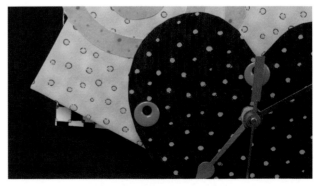

A folded-over edge is fast and clean.

Mounting the Clock Movement and Hands

Carefully pierce a hole in the center of the clock with sharp-pointed scissors or an awl. Use the scissors or a craft knife to open the hole wide enough to insert the stem. Push the stem from the back of the clock into the hole. Follow the manufacturer's instructions or refer to the illustration below. Attach the hour or little hand so it points to the 12 o'clock position. The position of the minute or big hand will be determined by the orientation of the rectangular slot on the stem.

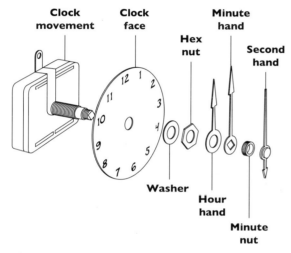

Assemble clock movement.

Hanging

Many clocks will hang nicely using the hanger that comes with the clock movement.

For other clocks, you'll need to build in a way to hang the clock.

For quilt or quilt-block style clocks, or clocks whose movement is off-center, attach a sleeve to the back, just as you would for a wall quilt (see page 47).

Use a sleeve just like on a quilt.

Another option is to sew or glue on a serrated picture hanger.

Buy serrated picture hangers at a hardware or art supply store.

Some clocks fit on a small easel or plate holder so you can display them on a table, dresser, or desk.

A variety of easels are available.

shaped clocks

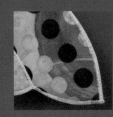

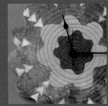

If you can cut it out, you can make it into a clock. From simple geometric designs to your favorite animals, these clocks are the perfect gifts for people with specific interests. Once you start thinking about it, ideas will appear everywhere.

What You'll Need

- Assorted yellow fabric scraps for butterfly wings
- Purple fabric for butterfly body: 2˝ × 9˝
- Scraps of contrasting fabric for hour markers
- Backing fabric: 19˝ × 13˝
- Heavyweight fast2fuse stiff interfacing, 28˝ wide: ⅜ yard
- Clock hands (5˝)
- Clock movement (⅜˝ stem)
- Paper-backed fusible web: 2˝ × 9˝
- Craft wire or chenille stems for antennae
- Cording or Iron-On Ribbon (see Resources)
- Pliers for bending wire (optional)

How-Tos

See pages 10–19 for basic techniques.

cut out the fast2fuse

Cut:

- 1 butterfly using the pattern on pullout 2 at the back of the book. Cut the pattern as one piece following the outermost edges.

make the butterfly

1. Iron the backing fabric to the butterfly. Trim to size using the fast2fuse as a guide.

2. Cut out the fabrics for the wings using the patterns on pullout 2 at the back of the book. Each piece allows for a little overlap.

3. Arrange all the pieces for the wings, overlapping the edges, as indicated, so no fast2fuse shows.

4. Iron the pieces in place, taking care not to iron over the uncovered fast2fuse.

5. Trace the butterfly body onto the paper side of fusible web.

6. Iron the fusible web to the back side of the body fabric, and trim following the line.

7. Remove the paper backing, and fuse the body in place.

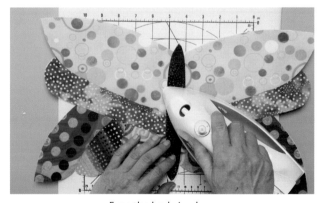

Fuse the body in place.

Arrange the wing pieces.

8. Satin stitch or couch cording over the edges of the wing pieces, starting with the vertical lines at the bottom of the butterfly. Then stitch the horizontal lines. Note: Iron-On Ribbon, if used instead of cording, can be fused in place; stitching over it ensures that it will stay in place.

Couch over cording.

9. Satin stitch around all the outside edges and the body.

easy!

Match the color of the thread to the background fabric when satin stitching; any fabric not completely covered with thread will blend in rather than stand out.

assemble the clock

1. Cut the hole for the stem of the clock movement.

2. Trace twelve ½˝ circles from the pattern on pullout 2 at the back of the book onto the paper side of fusible web. Iron the fusible web to the back side of the hour marker fabric. Cut out the circles. Remove the paper backing, and use the Hours Placement Guide on pullout 1 at the back of the book to arrange and fuse the hour markers in place.

3. Bend curlicues at the ends of 2 pieces of craft wire or chenille stems and cut them to length for the antennae. Glue them in place.

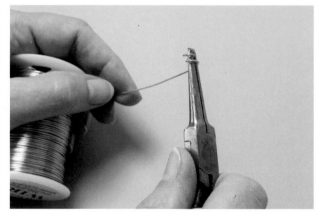

Bend wire for the antenna.

4. Mount the clock movement and attach the hands.

Variations

Now that you know how to make a shaped clock, design one in any shape you can imagine.

A. You can even make a clock that looks just like a clock. *Made by Patty Albin; clock face created using Husqvarna Viking 3D Embroidery software; other embroidery designs from Husqvarna Viking*

B. Round is just the shape for this dimpled golf ball and golf club. *Made by Teresa Stroin*

C. This teapot and teacup are a perfect match for a pendulum clock. *Made by Teresa Stroin*

D. Soft batting in this clock gives it an undulating look.

layered clocks

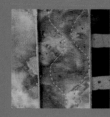

It's so easy! Layering clock pieces is a simple way to add depth and dimension to your clock.

What You'll Need

- [ ] Peach fabric: 12″ × 12″
- [ ] Yellow fabric: 10″ × 10″
- [ ] Pink/purple fabric: 7″ × 7″
- [ ] Light green fabric: 6″ × 6″
- [ ] Darker green fabric: 4″ × 4″
- [ ] Orange fabric: 4″ × 4″
- [ ] Backing fabric: 14″ × 14″

- [ ] Assorted fabric scraps for numbers and clock hands
- [ ] Heavyweight fast2fuse stiff interfacing, 28″ wide: ½ yard
- [ ] Clock hands (3½″)
- [ ] Clock movement (¾″ stem)
- [ ] Paper-backed fusible web: 7″ × 5″
- [ ] Plain copier paper or manila folder

How-Tos

See pages 10–19 for basic techniques.

cut out the fast2fuse

Use a compass to draw the circles, or use the circle patterns on pullout 1 at the back of the book.

Cut:

- [ ] 1 circle 11″ in diameter
- [ ] 1 circle 9″ in diameter
- [ ] 1 circle 6″ in diameter
- [ ] 1 circle 5″ in diameter
- [ ] 2 circles 3″ in diameter

make the circles

1. If you want a painted-edge finish, paint the edges of the fast2fuse now. The edges of this clock are painted with metallic gold paint.

2. Iron the backing fabric to the 11″ circle. Trim to size using the fast2fuse as a guide.

fun!

Make your layers stand out by painting the edges with a contrasting color.

3. Iron the top fabrics to all the circles. Trim to size using the fast2fuse as a guide.

4. If you plan to quilt the circles, do so now.

5. If you didn't paint the edges in Step 1, finish the edges of the circles now (see pages 16–17 for edge finishing options).

easy!

Quilt and finish the edges of your layers before you assemble the clock.

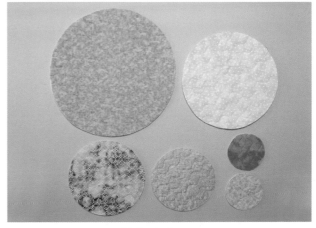

Make the layers.

make the numbers

1. Cut out the numbers from fast2fuse. Draw your own numbers or use the number patterns on pullout 1 at the back of the book.

2. Iron the fabrics to the right side of all the numbers. Trim to size using the fast2fuse as a guide.

3. Finish the edges.

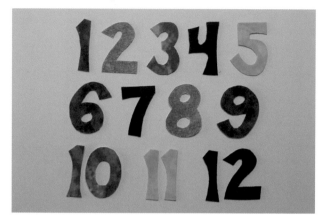

Make the numbers.

fast!

Use a craft knife with a fresh blade to cut out the numbers and trim the fabric to size.

make the hands

1. Trace the hands pattern on pullout 2 at the back of the book onto the paper side of fusible web. Cut out the hands, leaving ¼″ beyond the drawn line.

2. Iron the fusible web onto the back side of the fabric for the hands.

3. Trim on the drawn line.

4. Fuse the fabric to a piece of paper. Plain copier paper or a manila folder provides stability without adding much weight.

5. Glue the clock hands to the back side of the paper-backed fabric.

6. Cut out a small red dot (use fabric, felt, paper, or craft foam—whatever is handy) and glue it to the end of the second hand.

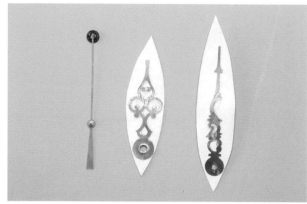

Make the hands.

easy!

Buy a clock movement with a pendulum so you can add yet another circle to your circles clock.

assemble the clock

1. Find the center of the 11″ circle and cut the hole for the stem of the clock movement.

2. Place the 9″ circle on the 11″ circle (note that it is not centered), mark the stem hole and cut it out.

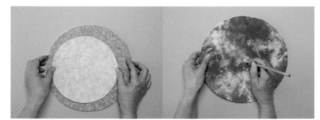

Place the 9″ circle on the 11″ circle, turn over, and mark the stem hole.

3. In a similar manner, place, mark, and cut the stem holes for the 6″ and 5″ circles.

4. Glue all the layers together, lining up the stem holes. Place the two 3″ circles as shown in the photo (see page 24). Use scraps of fast2fuse to separate and maintain space between the edges of layers when they overlap and aren't resting completely on a base circle.

5. Use the Hours Placement Guide on pullout 1 at the back of the book to arrange the numbers around the edge of the clock. Glue them in place. Use a scrap of fast2fuse to hold the number 10 together since only the 0 rests on the clock.

Use a scrap of fast2fuse to hold the 10 together.

6. Mount the clock movement and attach the hands.

Variations

Layers make the difference in these clocks.

A. Layers of fast2fuse and pattern-on-pattern fabric give this clock its sophisticated look. Curvy strips of fast2fuse are painted with metallic fabric paint and glued to the clock in **waves.** *Fabric provided by Timeless Treasures*

B. This plaid bear is made of two layers held together by the button eyes. *Made by Kiera Lofgreen*

C. A small dart in each outer petal gives this clock its curved shape. The layers give it depth and dimension.

A

B

C

dimensional layered clocks

For an attention-getting timepiece that literally jumps out at you, add space between the layers of your clock.

What You'll Need

- ☐ Black-and-white checked fabric for large square: 1 fat quarter
- ☐ Yellow-green print for small square: 1 fat quarter
- ☐ Red print for heart: 1 fat quarter
- ☐ Orange print for spirals: 7″ × 7″
- ☐ Backing fabric: ½ yard (includes sleeve)
- ☐ Heavyweight fast2fuse stiff interfacing, 28″ wide: ¾ yard
- ☐ Clock hands (5″)
- ☐ Clock movement (⅜″ stem)
- ☐ Paper-backed fusible web: ⅓ yard
- ☐ 1″-wide hook-and-loop tape: about 2″
- ☐ 1″ Styrofoam or craft foam: 6″ × 6″
- ☐ Manila folder or heavy cardstock
- ☐ Embellishments to mark the hours: 4

How-Tos

See pages 10–19 for basic techniques.

cut out the fast2fuse

Cut:

- ☐ 1 square 11″ × 11″
- ☐ 1 square 8½″ × 8½″
- ☐ 1 heart using the pattern on pullout 1 at the back of the book

make the shapes

1. Iron backing fabric to each fast2fuse shape. Trim to size using the fast2fuse as a guide.

2. Cut the fabric for the front of each shape ¾″ larger on all sides, and iron the fabric to the front of each shape.

3. Follow the Folded-Over Edge instructions on page 47 to wrap the fabric to the back for a clean edge.

Prepare the pieces.

make the spirals

1. Copy the spiral pattern on pullout 1 at the back of the book onto the manila folder or cardstock and trim to 7″ × 7″.

2. Iron 7″ × 7″ square of the fusible web onto the back.

3. Remove the paper backing and fuse the fabric square to the unmarked side of the manila folder or cardstock.

4. Cut out the spirals by cutting around the outer edge of the circle along the solid line. Then cut into to the center on the solid line and back out on the dotted line. This will give you 2 spirals.

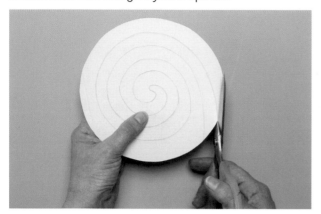

Cut the spirals.

assemble the clock

1. Either make a hanging sleeve and sew it to the back of the large square (see page 47 for sleeve construction) or plan to glue a serrated picture hanger on the back when you finish (see page 19).

fast!

A serrated picture hanger is a quick way to hang a clock when you can't use the hanger that comes with the clock movement.

2. Glue the Styrofoam square to the back of the finished small square. Then glue the unit to the large square. Refer to the photo on page 28 for placement.

3. Cut a hole in the heart for the stem of the clock movement.

4. Temporarily mount the clock movement in the heart. Determine the placement of the heart on the small square and mark the outline of the clock movement with masking tape.

Mark the placement of the clock movement.

5. Cut and glue one side of the hook-and-loop tape to the back of the clock movement. Don't cover the battery or the time-setting dial. Glue the other part of the hook-and-loop tape on the small square.

Place and glue the hook-and-loop tape.

6. Glue embellishments on the heart to mark the hours.

7. When all the glue is dry, mount the clock movement in the heart and press it into place on the small square.

easy!

The clock movement is attached with hook-and-loop tape so it can be removed to set the time and replace the battery.

8. Position and glue the spirals in place.

9. Attach the clock hands.

Variations

Now that you know the trick of attaching your clock movement with hook-and-loop tape, you can take your clocks to even greater dimensions.

A. These fast2fuse shapes are painted with metallic paints. One triangle was covered with a mesh weave for texture, and subtle patterns were added to the other triangles with metallic gold paint.

B. Bright solids stand out against the black background in this multipart clock.

C. Assemble your favorite spring flowers to make a collage clock.

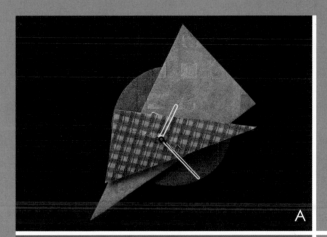

A

B

C

house clocks

From your dream house to the birdhouse, you can go cuckoo with a house clock. Be your own architect!

What You'll Need

- ☐ Brown print fabric: 1 yard (or several different fabrics to total 1 yard)
- ☐ Green scraps for leaves and stems
- ☐ Paper or pretreated fabric sheet for clock face: 8½″ × 11″
- ☐ Heavy white fabric, optional (6″ × 6″)
- ☐ Lace: 1 yard
- ☐ Heavyweight fast2fuse stiff interfacing, 28″ wide: 1 yard
- ☐ Clock hands (2¾″)
- ☐ Clock movement (⅜″ stem)

- ☐ Paper-backed fusible web, 17″ wide: ⅓ yard
- ☐ Brown and green acrylic or fabric paint
- ☐ Buttons: ½″ (11 for window, 9 for flower centers), 1″ (9 for flowers)
- ☐ Small bird
- ☐ Lightweight wood: 1 piece ½″ × ¼″ × 7¾″
- ☐ Heavy yellow thread
- ☐ Rotary cutter with pinking blade or narrow green rickrack for stems
- ☐ Hot-melt glue and glue gun

How-Tos

See pages 10–19 for basic techniques.

cut out the fast2fuse

Cut:

- ☐ 2 house shapes using the pattern on pullout 1 at the back of the book. Cut out the window on one for the house front; on the other, trim ⅛″ off each side and the bottom so it can slip inside the house for the back.
- ☐ 3 rectangles 4″ × 8″ for the house sides and bottom
- ☐ 2 rectangles 5″ × 8″ for the roof

make the house

1. Sew a 4″ × 8″ rectangle to each side of the house front and sew the roof rectangles together along the short sides. Sew the pieces together, as shown, using a wide zigzag stitch (length = 2; width = 5), which allows the pieces to bend.

Sew pieces together with wide zigzag.

2. If you want a painted-edge finish, paint the edges of the fast2fuse brown.

3. Iron the selected fabrics to one side of all the fast2fuse pieces. Trim to size using the fast2fuse as a guide. Cut out the window.

4. Iron the fabrics to the other side of all the pieces. Trim to size using the fast2fuse as a guide.

5. If you plan to quilt the pieces, do so now.

6. If you didn't paint the edges in Step 2, finish the edges now (see pages 16–17 for edge finishing options).

fun!

Cover gap with strip of contrasting fabric.

easy!

Quilt and finish the edges of your pieces before you assemble the clock.

make the roof

1. Bend the roof to the angle that matches the peak of the house.

2. Glue lace to the edge of the roof.

easy!

To stiffen the lace trim, paint it with Mod Podge or acrylic gel medium.

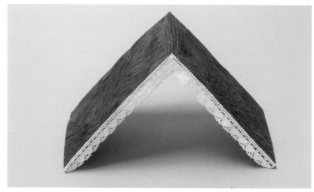

Make the roof.

make the clock face

1. Copy the clock face from pullout 1 at the back of the book onto paper or the pretreated fabric sheet.

2. To prevent the darker house fabric from shadowing through, fuse the clock face to a piece of fast2fuse or to a piece of heavy white fabric.

3. Mark the center of the clock face and cut the hole for the stem of the clock movement.

4. Place the clock face on the front of the house using the placement guide from the house pattern for reference. Mark and cut out the stem hole in the front of the house.

5. Glue or fuse the clock face to the clock.

make the flower garden

1. Iron fusible web to the back of the stem and leaf fabric.

2. Use a decorative pinking blade to cut the stems or use narrow green rickrack.

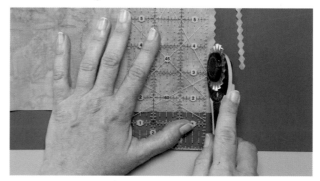

Use a pinking blade to make stems.

3. Cut out 18 leaves. Use the patterns on pullout 2 at the back of the book or create your own leaf shapes.

4. Arrange the stems and leaves, then fuse them to the sides and front of the house.

5. Stack buttons for flowers, then sew or glue it to the house.

6. Sew or glue the buttons around the window.

7. Paint the remaining lace green and set it aside to dry.

assemble the clock

1. Glue the 4″ × 8″ bottom in place. Place the house on top of the bottom piece so the fast2fuse edge of the bottom is visible. The green lace grass will later cover the exposed edge.

The wood stabilizes the house.

2. Hot glue the piece of wood to the back of the clock, as shown.

3. Mount the clock movement and attach the hands.

4. Glue the bird in the window.

5. Glue the green-painted lace grass around the bottom of the house.

6. Slip the house back piece inside the house in front of the wood support. Do not glue this piece in place; it will need to be removed to set the time and replace the batteries.

7. Place the roof on the top of the house and glue it to the front and sides of the house (not the back).

Variations

Take liberties with the basic cuckoo clock pattern. Change the roof, change the look—make it your own.

A. Bright primary colors and hearts make this the perfect clock for a child's room.

B. Made from felted wool, this clock is warm and cozy.

A B

scrapbook clocks

Get your photos out of the box and onto the wall. Here's a practical way to display your favorite photo memories and swap them out whenever you like.

Dog photos by Franki Kohler

What You'll Need

- ☐ 3–5 coordinating fabrics for pieced front and clock face: ½ yard total
- ☐ Backing fabric: ¾ yard (includes sleeve)
- ☐ Binding fabric: 5½″ × 24″
- ☐ Rose fabric scraps for accents
- ☐ Heavyweight fast2fuse stiff interfacing, 28″ wide: ¾ yard

- ☐ Clock hands (3″)
- ☐ Clock movement (⅜″ stem)
- ☐ Paper-backed fusible web, 17″ wide: ¾ yard
- ☐ Silver metallic acrylic or fabric paint
- ☐ 22–24 spiral paper clips: ⅞″
- ☐ Bugle and nibblette beads
- ☐ Rotary cutter with pinking blade

easy!

Pick closely related coordinating fabrics when selecting fabrics for the front of the clock. Different fabrics provide variety without being too distracting.

easy!

The frame templates are for 4″ × 6″ photos, but you can make them different sizes if you have different sizes of photos.

How-Tos

See pages 10–19 for basic techniques.

cut out the fast2fuse

Cut:

- ☐ 1 rectangle 22″ × 16″ for the background
- ☐ 5 frames using the template on pullout 2 at the back of the book

fast!

Use a sharp craft knife to cut out the frames.

make the background

1. Use the diagram below to cut out and sew the fabric pieces together with a ¼″ seam allowance to create the pieced background.

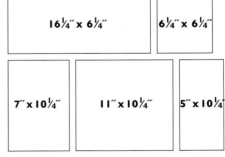

Construct the background. Note: Dimensions are the size to cut and include seam allowances.

2. Iron the backing fabric to the 22″ × 16″ piece of fast2fuse.

3. Iron the pieced background to the fast2fuse.

4. If you plan to quilt the background, do so now.

5. Iron fusible web onto the back of the binding fabric. Use a decorative rotary cutter to cut 4 strips 1¼″ × 24″. Follow the directions on page 46 to apply the fused binding.

make the frames

1. Glue the beads to the cutout frames using tacky glue. Put more beads in the corners than in the center of each side.

2. When the glue is dry, paint the frames with silver metallic paint. Be sure to paint the inside and outside edges. Apply the paint liberally.

Glue beads to the frames, then paint.

easy!

Use any color of beads for the frames. They will be painted, so use what you have or look for a bargain.

cut out the accent pieces

1. Iron fusible web to the back of the rose accent fabric.

2. Cut 2 strips 1¼″ × 4¼″ and 1 strip 1½″ × 5½″.

3. Cut out 4 circles 1⅛″ in diameter from the rose accent fabric. Use a compass or the circle pattern on pullout 1 at the back of the book.

easy!

Display your clock on a table using a small easel.

assemble the clock

1. Cut out an 8″ × 8″ square of fusible web and iron it to the back of the clock face fabric. Trim the clock face to 7″ × 7″.

2. Paint the clock hands silver (see page 8).

3. Refer to the photo on page 36 and arrange all the pieces on the background.

4. When you are happy with the placement, fuse the clock face and rose accents in place.

5. Use a very thin line of tacky glue to glue the frames and the spiral paper clips in place. **Do not glue the top edge of the frame.**

6. When the glue is dry, find the center of the clock face and cut a hole for the stem of the clock movement.

7. Make a sleeve and sew it to the back of the clock (see page 47).

8. Mount the clock movement and attach the hands.

9. Slip your favorite photos into the frames.

Variations

Scrapbook clocks are easy to make in any style. Make frames so that pictures can be swapped out, or permanently attach the picture to the background.

A. Extra-large crayons were scanned and printed on cardstock for the hands of this fun clock.

B. Hawaiian shirt fabric is the perfect background for tropical vacation pictures.

C. Dimensional flowers add a colorful touch to this feline portrait.

quilt-block clocks

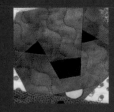

Quilting is such a "time-honored" tradition. Tie a room together with a quilt-block clock to complement the bedspread or a wallhanging. Recreate a block from your favorite project or vintage quilt, or salvage one from a well-loved family favorite.

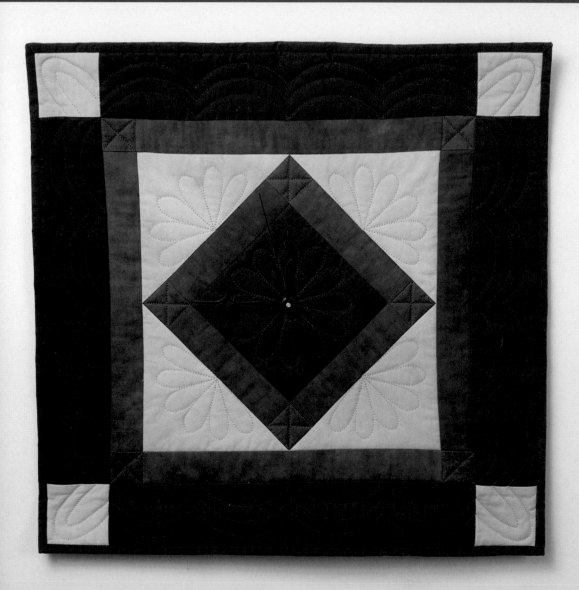

What You'll Need

- ☐ Rust fabric: ½ yard (includes binding)
- ☐ Teal fabric: ¼ yard
- ☐ Aqua fabric: ¼ yard
- ☐ Red fabric: ⅛ yard

- ☐ Backing fabric: ¾ yard (includes sleeve)
- ☐ Heavyweight fast2fuse stiff interfacing or batting (28″ wide): ¾ yard
- ☐ Clock hands (3½″–4½″)
- ☐ Clock movement (⅜″ stem)

How-Tos

See pages 10–19 for basic techniques.

cut out the fabrics

Rust

Cut:

- ☐ 1 square 5½″ × 5½″ for the center square
- ☐ 4 strips 13¾″ × 3″ for the outer borders

Teal

Cut:

- ☐ 4 strips 5½″ × 1¾″ for the first inner border
- ☐ 4 strips 11¼″ × 1¾″ for the second inner border

Aqua

Cut:

- ☐ 2 squares 6¼″ × 6¼″ in half diagonally for the triangles
- ☐ 4 squares 3″ × 3″ for the outer corner squares

Red

Cut:

- ☐ 8 squares 1¾″ × 1¾″ for the inner border squares

easy!

Follow the pressing instructions and all your seams will nest for easy alignment.

make the block

Refer to the Block Assembly Diagram on page 42.

1. Sew 2 first inner border strips to opposite sides of the center square using a ¼″ seam allowance. Press toward the border strips.

2. Sew red squares to the ends of the other 2 first inner border strips. Press toward the border strips.

3. Sew the strips to the center unit, nesting the seams. Press toward the border.

4. Pin and sew 2 aqua triangles to opposite sides of the center unit. Be careful not to stretch the bias edges of the triangles. Press toward the triangles.

5. Sew the remaining triangles to the center unit. Press toward the triangles.

6. Sew 2 second inner border strips to opposite sides of the center unit. Press toward the border strips.

7. Sew red squares to the ends of the other 2 second inner border strips. Press toward the border strips.

8. Sew the strips to the center unit, nesting the seams. Press toward the border.

9. Sew 2 outer border strips to opposite sides of the center unit. Press toward the outer border strips.

10. Sew aqua squares to the ends of the other 2 outer border strips. Press toward the border strips.

11. Sew the strips to the center unit, nesting the seams. Press toward the border.

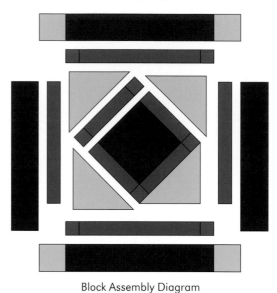

Block Assembly Diagram

quilt and bind the block

1. Cut one 22″ × 22″ square of batting or fast2fuse and one of backing fabric.

2. Layer the backing, the batting or fast2fuse, and the pieced block. Baste or fuse.

3. Quilt by hand or machine. Use the quilting designs on pullout 2 at the back of the book or design your own quilting pattern.

4. Trim and square up the quilted block.

easy!

Align the center quilting pattern so the petals mark the hours.

5. Finish the edges with traditional or fused binding (see page 46).

assemble the clock

1. Make a sleeve to sew to the back of the clock (see page 47).

2. Find the center of the quilt block and cut a hole for the stem of the clock movement.

3. Mount the clock movement and attach the hands.

Variations

Many styles of quilt blocks are perfect as clocks.

A. With a Mariner's Compass-style block. *Made by Wendy Hill*

B. Piece or appliqué your favorite bear pattern. *Peaceable Bear pattern by Ruth B. McDowell (see Resources on page 48)*

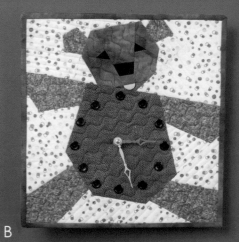

A | B

more ideas

Look out—once you start making fabric clocks, you'll be surprised where your imagination and energy take you. Here are some more ideas to inspire you.

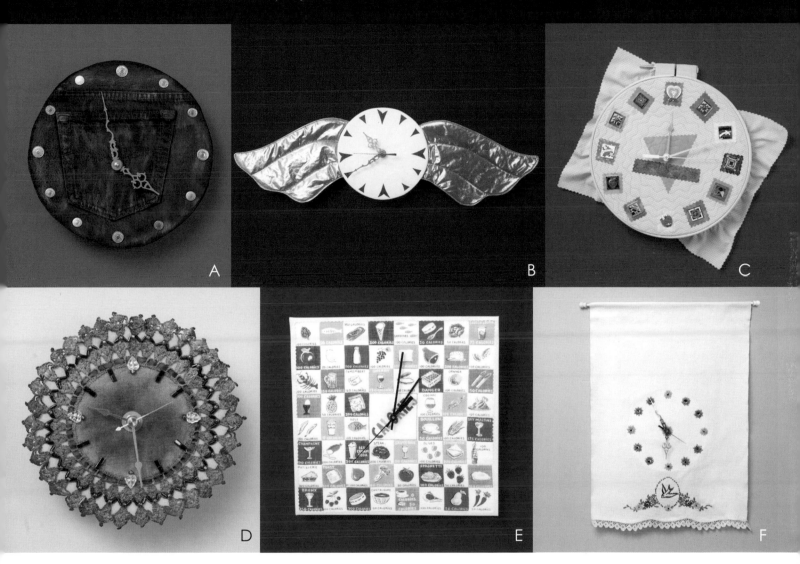

A. Can't bear to part with your beloved old jeans? Make them into a clock, and mark the hours with the studs from the button fly.

B. Time flies when you're quilting this winged clock. The gold lamé wings are quilted with batting inside.

C. Ever wonder what to do with the quilting hoop you don't use anymore? Not only can you put an unused hoop to work, you can display your quilt pins as well.

D. Paint an old linen and lace doily with fabric paint and add some sparkle with ribbon and beads.

E. A treasured old hankie finds new life as a clock. *Made by Franki Kohler*

F. What a great way to display a one-of-a-kind embroidered tea towel! *Bluebird embroidery by Eleanor Epperson; additional daisy embroidery by Yvonne Longsworth*

Fabric-Printed Clocks

Printing on fabric with an inkjet printer is a great way to create a clock. See Resources on page 48 for books and supplies for printing your own fabric.

A   B

C   D

A. Buttons and spools of thread were scanned and the images combined for this sewing-themed clock.

B. A kaleidoscope effect in photo-editing software was used to create this twelve-sided shape.

C. A variety of photos were printed on fabric and stitched together. Each photo depicts how the clock-maker would like to be spending her day. *Made by Cyndy Lyle Rymer*

D. Photos from a trip to Alaska were printed in a Log Cabin block arrangement.

Paper and Fabric Clocks

For even more options, combine paper and fabric, or just use paper. Paper gives you even more colors and patterns to choose from, and you can work with it just as you do fabric.

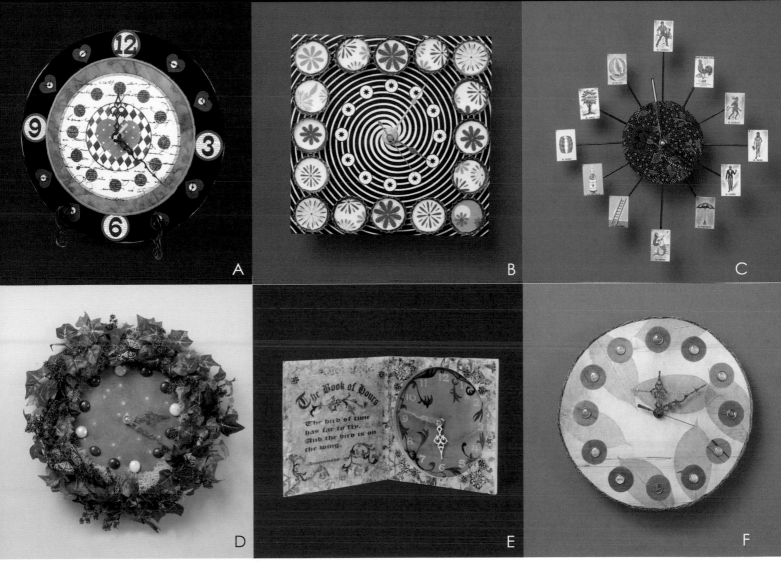

A. Fabric and paper are used interchangeably in this clock. *Made by Sue Astroth*

B. The black-and-white spiral design was printed on paper with an inkjet printer and surrounded with fabric-lined bottle caps. *Made by Becky Goldsmith*

C. Lotería tickets from a Mexican bingo-style game are used to mark the hours. Painted skewers fasten the tickets to the clock center. *Made by Stacy Chamness*

D. One stop at the craft store provided all the supplies for this botanical clock, including scrapbook paper, polished rocks, greenery, and butterflies. *Made by Rose Wright*

E. This clock was made from a blank board book (see Resources on page 48). Decorative and tissue papers were layered and glued with acrylic gel medium. The saying was printed on silk and glued to the layered background with acrylic gel medium.

F. A scrapbook store supplied a treasure trove of ideas for this clock, including scrapbook paper, skeleton leaves, scrapbooking brads to mark the hours, and braided cord for the outside edge.

finishing

Traditional Quilt Binding

1. Cut 1¼″-wide strips of binding fabric—enough to go around the clock plus 10″. If you need to join strips together, join them with a diagonal seam.

2. Cut the starting end on a 45° angle and fold under ¼″. Match the raw edge of the binding with the raw edge of the clock.

3. Stitch using a ¼″ seam allowance. Stop ¼″ from the corner and backstitch.

4. Fold the fabric straight up so the binding forms a 45° angle.

5. Fold the binding straight down, matching the raw edges. Backstitch, and sew to the next corner. Repeat the process on the remaining corners.

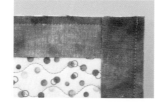

6. Sew to within 3″ of where you started.

7. Trim the end of the binding so that you have at least 1″ to completely overlap the starting end.

8. Finish sewing the binding to the clock. Then fold the binding to the back, fold the raw edge under ¼″, and fuse or hand stitch it down.

Fused Binding

1. Measure the longest side of the clock.

2. Cut a rectangle of fabric 5½″ wide × 2″ longer than the longest side of the clock. If you are binding curves, be sure to cut the fabric on the bias.

3. Iron fusible web to the back of the fabric.

4. Remove the paper backing and cut the fused fabric into 1¼″-wide strips with a rotary cutter. A decorative-edge blade adds a nice touch.

5. Finger-press the binding strips in half so you know where the center is.

6. Line up a binding strip so the halfway crease is on the edge of the clock. Protect your ironing board with an appliqué pressing sheet and fuse the binding strip to the front of the clock. Add a second strip to the opposite side of the quilt.

7. Fold the binding strips to the back and press in place. Trim the excess binding even at the corners.

8. Repeat Step 6 on the 2 other sides.

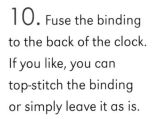

9. Fold the corners under at a 45° angle.

10. Fuse the binding to the back of the clock. If you like, you can top-stitch the binding or simply leave it as is.

fun!

Use decorative edges on fused binding for a different look.

Folded-Over Edge

1. Fuse the backing fabric to the fast2fuse and cut it to size using the fast2fuse as a guide.

2. Cut the fabric for the front of the clock or clock piece about ¾″ larger on all sides than the finished size.

3. Center the fabric so that equal amounts of fabric hang over the edge of the fast2fuse, and fuse in place.

4. Cut ½″-wide strips of paper-backed fusible web and iron them to the edges of the fabric.

5. Fold the fabric to the back and press in place, fusing the fabric to the backing. For corners, trim or tuck in fabric as needed. Clip curves as needed.

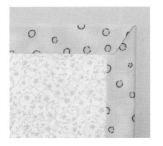

Hanging Sleeve

A hanging sleeve is a good way to hang a clock when you can't use the metal hanger that comes with the clock movement.

1. Cut a piece of fabric 6″× the width of the clock.

2. Fold under the short edges ½″ twice. Stitch.

3. Fold the fabric **wrong** sides together lengthwise. Sew the long edge with a ¼″ seam. Press the seam open.

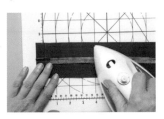

4. Pin the sleeve in place and hand sew it to the backing. Be sure to sew down the short ends so the hanging rod goes into the sleeve and not between the sleeve and the clock.

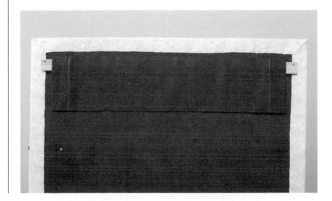

About the Author

Sewing has been a constant in Lynn Koolish's life ever since her mother taught her to sew when she was old enough to sit at a sewing machine. Lynn has worked in a number of career fields but was thrilled to finally settle down with quilting in the 1990s.

Also by Lynn Koolish

Lynn works in a variety of styles and loves experimenting with new ideas, materials, and techniques. She works full-time editing quilting books and teaches a variety of surface design and quilting classes. Her quilts have appeared in books, magazines, and local and national quilt shows.

Resources

Clock movements and hands
Check your local craft or woodworking shop or order from www.rockler.com www.walnuthollow.com

fast2fuse
Check your local quilt shop or order from www.ctpub.com

Blank board books
Check your local craft or scrapbooking shop or order from www.ctpub.com

Pretreated fabric sheets for inkjet printers
Check your local quilt shop or order from www.colortextiles.com or www.printedtreasures.com

Peaceable Bear pattern page 42
Available from Ruth McDowell at www.ruthbmcdowell.com

Iron-On Ribbon by Kreinik
Check your local quilt or craft shop or order from www.kreinik.com

Books
Printing on fabric: *More Photo Fun* by the Hewlett-Packard Company with Cyndy Rymer and Lynn Koolish

Quilting basics: *Start Quilting with Alex Anderson* by Alex Anderson

Fusing: *Fusing Fun* by Laura Wasilowski

For a list of other fine books from C&T Publishing, ask for a free catalog:

C&T Publishing, Inc.
P.O. Box 1456
Lafayette, CA 94549
(800) 284-1114
Email:ctinfo@ctpub.com
Website: www.ctpub.com

For sewing and quilting supplies:

Cotton Patch Mail Order
3405 Hall Lane, Dept. CTB
Lafayette, CA 94549
(800) 835-4418
(925) 283-7883
Email: quiltusa@yahoo.com
Website: www.quiltusa.com